Busy Woman to Business Woman

WALKING BY FAITH

BUSY WOMAN TO BUSINESS WOMAN

WALKING BY FAITH

"Now FAITH is confidence in what we hope for and assurance about what we do not see."

Hebrews 11:1 (NIV)

This book was awesome and I could not put it down! It was easy to read and follow. It was also thought provoking and inspiring. What I was able to gain, beyond the mechanical and technical aspects of starting a business, were applications of moral and spiritual concepts. The information was relevant for today, but it provoked you to look in to your own history for clues to your own destiny. The prayers and reflections, at the end of the chapters, gave me a moment to pray, reflect, and organize my thoughts without having to put the book down; and, I did pray! Sharing this information along with your personal journey, your fears and your success was encouraging. It gave me the motivation to get "It" together! I pray that it inspires others, as it did me!

CRYSTAL TRAMMELL

Acknowledgements

I dedicate this book to my mother, Minister Doris Lewis-Marshall who taught me how to always stand up for what was right, rely on God to back me up and just believe. As a mother, the effects of her Godly wisdom and experiences has resulted into a passion for giving and I learned that giving was not limited to financial monetary gain. I am grateful that I have the opportunity to witness and release to many the powerful impact God has made in my life. My mother's ministering of love, integrity, kindness, character, honesty, grace and dedication has encouraged many lifetime goals and accomplishments, in my life. As I continue to pursue the vision God has revealed for my future, her love will forever be sealed in my heart.

I am acknowledging the late Eddie Lee Marshall who fathered me from early childhood, until marriage, as one of his own. He instilled, in my memory, the importance of demanding respect, handling my financial affairs and focusing on my life and future. I love and thank God, for him. Loving all of my sisters, who can validate everything in this book from life lessons we learned growing up in the house together! Ladies, thank you for supporting me in ALL OF MY CRAZY and SUCCESSFUL business ventures. Thank you to Glenn, Cheryl, Liam, and Kellie who all play a special part in my life. I am thankful to my Mother- in – Love for helping me bring my dream to life.

I would like to make an honorable mention to my darling grandmother, Minnie Lewis, for her dedication, prayers and faith. Finally, to my wonderful and supportive husband Larry and awesome son Cole, the planning, scheduling and deadlines would not be possible without your unconditional love for me. I am so blessed to have you guys, as my personal cheer team. And, to my Cole's Castle Kings & Queens, I thank you for allowing Mrs. Catrina to be a part of your lives! I love you all!

Table of Contents

Preface

I was the little girl who played dress up in my mom's heels, dragged her briefcase around the house and pretended to be a business woman. Unknowingly, I was setting the stage for my future, as a successful African American Business Woman from Detroit. In society, Olympic gymnasts begin taking gymnastics at age two, famous singers start singing at age three and NFL players begin hiking footballs, in youth leagues, by the age of five. The impressionable age of four and five were positive links to my adventurous curiosity. Life's everyday rituals became stepping stones into my future. Education and fashion were two passions that fit hand and glove, in my life. I enjoyed doing things that made me feel and look successful. I also began to apply these emotions and deeds, to my everyday life. The results are my roles as an entrepreneur and personal stylist.

Humble beginnings often left little room for financial growth. I often worked for little or nothing as a teen. Volunteering helped me to expand my hands on knowledge, In many areas of professionalism. The application of skills and wisdom began to produce an eagerness to grow and know more, as I sought different levels of interest. Some of those things I even had to do for free, at first, like babysitting and assisting in my middle and high school office. I soon learned that when you do it for free, God can turn it into a profitable business opportunity for you. I went from just being BUSY to being **PRODUCTIVE IN LIFE**.

Today's youth are faced with many struggles and challenges. Socially, I recognized the lack and application of positive life skills. This inspired me to pray, study, research and nurture a spirit of giving back what was so unselfishly given to me. Reaching out to share my gifts and talents has been rewarding. I am grateful to have the opportunity to witness and be in the midst of the impact God has made in our lives. I wrote this book with the next generation in mind to show them how they can take their life skills and lessons of today and turn them into profitable business ventures in the very near future. I'm not talking in their 20's or 40's, but I mean now in their teens and adolescence to begin building a bright future for themselves and their families. I also pray that this information could help a retiree, widower or empty nester begin to find and develop their purpose and calling in life. For, it's never too late to go from **Busy Woman to Business Woman!**

The Plan

Jeremiah 29:11- "For I know the plans I have for you, declares the LORD, plans to prosper you and not to harm you, plans to give you hope and a future." (NIV) You must set a realistic goal, in your life, that focus on your accomplishments and don't stop trying until you succeed. But, how can you, if you are **ALWAYS** so **BUSY?** First, you must devise a plan to declare freedom from being a **BUSYBODY!**

Here are 3 steps:

1. ***PRAY:*** To successfully go from BW2BW, it is always best to pray and seek God's counsel in **ALL** your decision making. Start your day off, in prayer alone or with your family and God will direct and keep you focused. Building a trusting relationship with God is vital and sharing intimate alone time is crucial. It's all right to ask God questions and expect answers that deliver change, in your life. He will direct your path and give you unmerited favor, while aligning your life to where you can enjoy it to the fullest. To accurately hear from God, you have to be still and quiet enough to listen and receive. He will even respond through people, tests, and occasions that will often times shock you and will even let you know it was Him. Yes, challenges will

arise, but His grace and mercy will cover you, no matter what storm may come your way. My God has never failed me yet and definitely answers my prayers, when I ask for direction, both in a minor or major situation. Over the years, I have learned that prayer changes things and those times when it seemed like it was taking longer than normal, God always showed up on time.

2. ***WRITE IT DOWN***: Whatever the IT is, write IT down and make IT plain on paper! This will release stress, on your brain, of having to remember what to do and give you more time to concentrate on the project rather than dwell over and over about IT. Your mind can only hold so much. A doctor's appointment, wedding, meeting, vacation, invention, car repair or church function, no matter what IT might be, the IT needs to go on a calendar not a mental rolodex. Don't try to internalize and hold everything in, because the one thing that slips your mind can cost you a deal, relationship or even a life. Phones have calendars built right in them and they can help you to keep track of upcoming events. Carry a cute little notebook in your purse and put some post it notes on your desk to help write things down. Remember, the old school pen and paper never really went out of style. Just like a teen with a diary, grab a notebook and begin to journal to God, so His secrets can begin to be revealed to you for His plan for your life. Be intimate with God and write Him a love letter and don't be surprised when He writes you one back!

3. **_PRIORITIZE_**: You should always plan ahead to figure out what your next step will be and to help take the load off yourself. If you have to get your children ready for the week and they are small, prepare early. Pack diaper bags, briefcases and lunches at night. Grocery shop for the month and iron clothes on a Sunday night for the entire week. Even, your own clothes should be ready the night before, to help eliminate early morning rush hour at home. That is the hour you wake up and everything goes wrong at the same time. The baby throws up, the car won't start, you can't find your keys and you need that extra 15 minutes of sleep. If you have older children, it's time for them to share the responsibilities. So, delegate chores and allow them to earn a weekly allowance. Now, some of you ladies might say I don't have any children yet! That's even better, because your preparation time will be less. You can still apply the same concepts, just do it only for you. Cut that make-up and glamour time in half and put down that phone! Instead listen to some music or inspirational teachings that will inspire you to get your day started off with a bang! When planning at night, it also will give you that extra prayer and physical exercise time in the morning! Choose things that can help your day start off positive and eliminate some of that day to day stress.

The truth is, when you have a plan for your life, it helps you to stay focused on your real purpose in life. The older you get, time and life becomes more precious. You begin to realize that it's time to get the ball rolling before life really passes me by.

Everyone is born with some type of talent and or gift that can be turned into a business, but everyone does not possess the drive and ambition to pursue these intuitions. So, if you are really ready to open that jewelry store, construction company or dive feet first into that business venture, let this guide you on your journey.

A TIME TO REFLECT

PICK A DAILY PRAYER TIME TO SPEND QUIET TIME WITH GOD AND STICK TO IT.

____6:00 AM	____12:00 NOON
____6:00 PM	____12:00 AM

TO DO LIST - WRITE DOWN ALL OF THE TASKS TO TAKE CARE OF, IN YOUR MIND, IN ORDER OF IMPORTANCE. (EX. PAY CABLE BILL/PICK UP CLEANERS/WEDDING NEXT MONTH)

1. _____
   _____
2. _____
   _____
3. _____
   _____

4. _____
   _____
5. _____
   _____

Don't overburden yourself. But, be realistic and honest with how much you can take on at a time.

WHAT ARE 3 THINGS THAT YOU CAN TACKLE, AT NIGHT, THAT WILL HELP YOUR MORNINGS RUN SMOOTHER?

1. _____
   _____
2. _____
   _____
3. _____
   _____

PRAYER

FATHER, HELP ME TO LEARN HOW TO SPEND MORE TIME IN PRAYER WITH YOU AND TO MAKE YOU A PRIORITY IN MY LIFE. REMOVE DISTRACTIONS FROM MY SIGHT AND PLACE MY PURPOSE AND DESTINY BEFORE ME TO PURSUE. FORGIVE ME FOR ANY THOUGHTS OR BEHAVIORS THAT DIDN'T EXEMPLIFY A LIFE OF CHRIST. IN JESUS NAME, AMEN.

Chapter Two

Transition & Balance

I remember, as a young child, going to school, bible studies, dance classes, Girl Scout meetings, fashion shows, events, vacations and many, many birthday parties. I am currently a wife, mother and business woman. I amazingly graduated from one level of life to another, and my schedule is still very fulfilling. Many ask me when I sleep. I often laugh and look back on my life and reminisce about how my parents took me to all these activities. I can only say it wasn't just about being busy, but I actually was developing skills to help me be the woman that I am today. I was preparing to become a productive woman with an assertive outlook on life that gave me the confidence that the stars and the sky was not the limit. I knew that I had a broader range of options. An educated woman, I was focused on reaching my full potential by using the knowledge that I have acquired over the years in a classroom setting. I am a Christian woman that walks, with the glory of the Lord as my strength, and exudes confidence wherever my feet lead me gaining wisdom from my elders. I thank God for all of the opportunities that I have experienced, in life so far, whether good or bad. I wouldn't change a thing, because it was simply my training and a testimony for someone in the near future.

One of the keys to having a balanced life, while transitioning from a teenager to adult, is to never lose sight of enjoyable activities from your youth. If you specialize in dance, join the dance team at your church or a local neighborhood organization. Utilize your gifts to help kids or teens, at a youth home, who never had the opportunity of learning how to dance. Your gifts are a blessing to have and could help save someone's life. My mother use to share stories to us about how dancing in high school was an outlet for her and literally helped to save and shape her life. With so many children failing and dropping out of school, consider becoming a tutor. If you are really good at academics, start a tutoring club to help children who can't read well or teach English as a second language. You can provide that extra help that they can't get from the school nor parents. And if writing is your craft, write a book, start a blog, become a ghostwriter for a music label, magazine, or even a writing coach. Titus 2:3-5 states " [3] Likewise, teach the older women to be reverent in the way they live, not to be slanderers or addicted to much wine, but to teach what is good. [4] Then they can urge the younger women to love their husbands and children, [5] to be self-controlled and pure, to be busy at home, to be kind, and to be subject to their husbands, so that no one will malign the word of God. (NIV) Remember, these are our future nurses, construction workers and government officials that must be taught and corrected just like we were. So, always show patience and empathy when working with our youth.

There are numerous classes and fun activities offered at local community colleges and churches such as archery, knitting, floral arrangements, jewelry making and photography for reasonable prices. These hobbies can spark an internal interest that can turn into a future profitable business. Offering your expertise in a charity is another great way of balance, by volunteering at a local soup kitchen or use your skills in the development of programs for a non-profit. Maybe supporting a cause you believe in like saving the wildlife, since you have a love for wild animals. Search out the history and foundation of the non-profit and attend a few of their meetings to make sure they share the same values as you. You can learn a lot and they may have a seat on the board for you to add your input and have a positive effect in today's world.

With the ever rising statistics of heart disease, strokes, dementia, and cancers in women, it's important that you exercise, rest and eat healthy. You can workout at home alone, but results are usually better when you get out and join a local gym. In most gyms, you have trainers or fitness experts that can guide and show you the areas of your body that needs the most work and toning. They will take your measurements, give you a tour and work out a reasonable price plan for you to handle that will keep you motivated in using your gym membership. Water aerobics are a good way to lose weight and stay cool, while exercising. Free hand weights, walking and aerobics stimulate all your muscles and keeps the blood properly flowing to your heart. Plus, the motivation that comes from seeing fifty or more people doing the same thing makes you want to join in on the fun. Remember to work at your own pace and be comfortable in your own skin, before trying to become the chin-up champion! Attending sporting events is another good way to put some recreation time in your life. Season tickets carry lots of perks and benefits and will give you a chance to meet the players, receive discounts on merchandise, attend private events and get a photo opportunity that will create a lifelong memory. This also gives you access to assign seating each time you attend the game and makes you feel as if you are part of the team.

Whether you are alone or with someone, make sure you recreate in some kind of way. It is possible for us to work ourselves into a frenzy, with a weekly forty to sixty hour career, and if not careful this life will pass us right on by. So, be mindful to enjoy the little things like treating yourself out to eat at least 2 times a month allowing someone to serve you for a change. Try to eat and drink healthy monitoring your sugars, fats and carbohydrates. Learn how to say "no thank you," to that extra piece of dessert and eat only enough. But, do stop in and visit that new sushi restaurant or yogurt bar, with the fresh fruit, and make sure you spend some personal time with yourself. Catching up on a movie, a walk in the park or by the water and just sitting on your front porch can be relaxing to many. Also we can't forget that manicure, pedicure and monthly eyebrow arch! We are so busy pleasing others that sometimes we forget how to please ourselves and what makes us happy. Take a small weekend getaway out of town, visit your downtown area or spend the night in a beautiful hotel and enjoy the sights. Treat yourself to room service, a spa treatment and catch a concert, while away. This is a quick and refreshing way to reenergize for the week ahead, but remember to rest also. Too often you need a vacation to rest from the vacation!

As a busy woman, there are things that we must do to stay relevant in this ever changing society. Keeping up with trends, what's hot and what's not are all good, but never stop investing in yourself. I find quiet daily times to study, journal and read my Bible. These daily instructions help keep me grounded and focused. My mother taught me that reading aloud would improve my speech and increase my vocabulary. It indeed has helped me to speak clearly, during a normal conversation, interviews, speaking engagements and even placing an order at a restaurant.

Companies require you to seek extra training from seminars and continuing education courses to stay abreast, of the ever changing workforce. Do not complain about trainings. Your employer evidently sees something in you that is worth investing in and desires to get the most out of their investment. Go ahead and register and begin to tap into that next level of expertise. After leaving, you will be on fire with a wealth of knowledge and a ton of great information that can inspire you to gear into a business woman.

Whatever you can do to help keep that balance in life from childhood to adulthood, do it. A lot of times, we become adults and get into the rush of the day that we forget what makes us happy or to do what we enjoy. You can devise a plan to enjoy your life each day and get fulfillment and joy out of helping others. The possibilities are endless, so where are you going to begin?

A TIME TO REFLECT

NAME SOME OF YOUR CHILDHOOD EXPERIENCES OR ACTIVITIES THAT HELPED MOLD YOU INTO THE INDIVIDUAL YOU ARE TODAY?

_____

_____

_____

_____

HOW IMPORTANT IS QUALITY TIME WITH YOURSELF?

_____

_____

_____

_____

_____

LIST SOME ACTIVITIES OR HOBBIES YOU ENJOY DOING ALONE OR
WITH SOMEONE.

_____

_____

_____

_____

_____

_____

WHAT YOUTH GROUP OR NON PROFIT CAN YOU PARTNER
WITH TO SHARE YOUR GIFTS & EXPERTISE?

_____

_____

_____

_____

_____

PRAYER

FATHER, THANK YOU FOR BLESSING ME WITH A MIND TO
WANT TO SERVE YOU WITH MY GIFTS AND MAKING TIME FOR
ME TO BALANCE THEM ALL, SO I CAN BE PRODUCTIVE AND
NOT JUST BUSY. THERE ARE SO MANY THAT HAVE NOT BEEN
TAPPED INTO YET AND I PRAY THAT THEY WILL ALL BE USED
TO EDIFY YOU AND BE A BLESSING TO OTHERS. I ALSO THANK
YOU FOR KEEPING ME ALL THESE YEARS AND POURING
EDUCATION AND EXPERIENCES INTO MY LIFE, WHILE
ALLOWING ME TO APPLY THAT KNOWLEDGE TO BETTER
MYSELF AND THOSE AROUND ME. KEEP MY HEART OPEN, SO I
CAN CONTINUE TO LEARN NEW AND EXCITING THINGS THAT
WILL BETTER MY CHARACTER AND INTEGRITY, AS A CHRISTIAN
WOMAN, ON A WALK WITH YOU. IN JESUS NAME, AMEN.

Chapter Three

Finding My Niche'

Businesses generally begin with ideas that come from a dream, thought or vision that God has placed in your spirit compelling you to bring it to life. It feels like your soul can't rest, until you do what you have been ordered to do. Like a boss who gives you directions and if you don't complete them you will get fired from that job and he will hire someone else to complete the task. For some, businesses are only a niche' turned into a way of life. What is a niche'? The Merriam-Webster dictionary states "that it's a place, employment, status or activity for which a person or thing is best fitted." Small ideas, like a lemonade stand on a corner by a child, can become a million dollar drink company or even a babysitting service can grow into a billion dollar childcare facility. How can that be? Just continue reading and you will be inspired and encouraged to reach beyond your ordinary mind and tap into the spirt realm in the business world. Be careful about running around sharing your precious vision with people, because everyone isn't on your team. God reminds us in John 10:10, "The thief comes only to steal, kill and destroy." (NIV) He will try everything he can to distract, intimidate or deter you from bringing your vision to pass.

When deciding on what type of business to go into, think of a service that could better your community and the world. Make sure you do something you actually enjoy doing, so that the novelty won't wear off so quickly.

For some, it's not easy and pretty scary to start a business from scratch. My niche' is children, because I helped my mom raise my three younger sisters since the age of twelve. My parents didn't make me do it. I just loved to help them and considered myself doing what big sisters are supposed to do. Watching my mother run a successful home daycare business, as a child, was also in my bloodline. But, I didn't know it would be one of my major businesses today. I'm a living witness of going from employee to employer. Personally, for me the first two months were very scary in my new business, especially after leaving a corporate place of employment with what I thought was a secure career. But, after 13 years, a college degree and an 80 hour check, I took a huge step out on faith to become an entrepreneur and had to realize that God was my source and not that job. I treated the new business as a ministry, because I was providing a service to parents that entrusted me with their most precious commodity, their children. I totally began to lean and dedicate my business to Him. This world makes it seem as if the job is necessary or the only way to make a living. I won't call any jobs names, but many people become like robots or enslaved to them when their vision and businesses are lying dormant inside of them. When you totally trust God, you can step out on faith, reach your goals, conquer the world and do anything. The Bible reminds us in Philippians 4:13, "[3] I can do all this through Him who gives me strength."(NIV) So, sit down and write your business plan, to do list, goals and get to IT. Put the remote, Facebook and Instagram down, get out of other people's lives and start making preparation for a new life for you and your family. You achieve your dreams and goals and don't apologize for being successful. The Bible clearly states these words in 3 John 1:2, "Dear friend, I pray that you may enjoy good health and that all may go well with you, even as your soul is getting along well."(NIV) We have to be positioned to prosper and ready to receive. When the blessings flow you want to be in your right mind to enjoy them. God wants you to run on the beach, travel, enjoy life and flourish in the fruits of your labor or you will end up leaving it for someone else!

Remember, if you don't get it right the first time keep trying. Never give up or give in. Maybe take a step back and reevaluate things and try again. Think about what was wrong and what can be fixed to help make it right. It usually takes about 2 years, for a good business to get off the ground and running good. You must work it and nurture it to get the kinks out and gain momentum and pretty soon it will begin to run itself.

A TIME TO REFLECT

IF YOU COULD WALK AWAY FROM YOUR JOB TODAY AND START YOUR OWN BUSINESS, WHAT WOULD BE YOUR TOP 3 CHOICES AND WHY?

1. _____
   _____
2. _____
   _____
3. _____
   _____

WHAT STEPS ARE YOU CURRENTLY TAKING TO MAKE THIS
DREAM A REALITY?

_____

_____

_____

_____

_____

PRAYER

*FATHER, I KNOW IN ORDER TO EAT I MUST WORK AND YOU
HAVE EQUIPPED ME WITH THE GIFT OF KNOWING HOW TO
FISH SO I CAN EAT FOR A LIFETIME. LET ME USE THESE
CREATIVE JUICES TO BRING MULTIPLE STREAMS OF INCOME
INTO MY LIFE. ALLOW ME TO MAKE MONEY, WHEN I SLEEP AT
NIGHT AND THE WISDOM TO KNOW HOW TO USE IT. IN JESUS
NAME, AMEN.*

Chapter Four

Leadership

As a business woman, there are a number of leadership qualities that helps your business run smooth. You must remain honest even if you see other people are doing the opposite. Your honesty will cause your level of character to go higher and line up with integrity. Having the trust of God, your consumers, staff and family is very important and vital, in the longevity of your business. Don't compromise, to make things a certain way and then go back to doing things another way. Follow your heart. It will line up with your thoughts and so will your actions.

Accepting too many assignments or deadlines is a risky way to live. Remember, you are only one person with one little brain up there that can handle a certain number of things at a time. Putting too much on your plate and becoming a YES girl is very dangerous. You agree to please the other person knowing you really don't want to do it or your schedule just won't allow you to accommodate them at this time. There we go with that **IT** again! Picking up too many activities, PTA clubs, church functions, work engagements or home activities can become overwhelming and cause a tremendous amount of stress which then brings on illnesses. Yes, you may be the best candidate for the job, but evaluate your current situation, before you over commit and stress yourself out as the deadline comes closer. Consistency is key and very important and you don't want to be the one who drops the ball, when it's passed to you to complete your goal. The

Bible says in Matthew 5:37 " All you need to say is simply 'Yes' or 'No'; anything beyond this comes from the evil one."(NIV) So, make sure you are honest with yourself and that you are not putting too many irons in the fire.

Learning how to say "I'm sorry" or "I apologize," even when you know you didn't do anything wrong, is something you will encounter as a business woman. The art of forgiveness is a challenge to some and a breeze to others. When you forgive someone for harming you whether it was intentional or non-intentional, you release a chain off of you that was keeping you in bondage. A lot of time blessings and things God wanted to send your way are put on hold, because of a simple grudge. Even in your mind, thoughts can flare up of what you would like to do to the other individual, but it's not our battle. Childhood hurts, teenage pains and adult offences can limit you from reaching your full potential in your career. Don't dwell in the past, but look up towards the future and know that in order to see God, you must first forgive those who offended you.

Confidentiality is key in a successful business. As a business woman you will be invited to private business meetings with talks of contracts about finances and developments, but be sure not to go and share vital information to your friends or family members about what your meetings are about. And, when you are trying to spread the good news, the devil can creep right in and sabotage the plan. Everyone can't be trusted and if you lose someone's trust, it's very hard to gain it back. You want people to be able to trust you with their deepest darkest secrets, if need be. Don't be a water faucet at the mouth and gossip and tell others' business. My mother always taught me, if you want to talk about someone, talk about yourself! Eliminate gossip, from your vocabulary!

Don't spend time putting your mouth on someone else's life or business and take a good look in the mirror and make sure that EVERYTHING you are doing is fine and in order! In Luke 6:42 it says, "How can you say to your brother, 'Brother, let me take the speck out of your eye,' when you yourself fail to see the plank in your own eye? You hypocrite, first take the plank out of your eye, and then you will see clearly to remove the speck from your brother's eye."(NIV) You can have an opinion about something, but that's all it is, an opinion and everyone has one. That's time and space, in your day that can be taken up with something else like prayer, praise and worship, creating a new business venture or sleep! Don't tear people down, because what goes around sure does come back around. Words can hurt, help and heal and there is life and death in the power of the tongue. Gossip has caused many people to commit suicide, fall into a life of drugs and sink into a life of depression. So, be careful to think before you speak and ask yourself am I using the Fruits of the Spirit, when I speak about this person or situation or am I doing this so I can just seem important?

In running a business, you often have to make a number of final decisions on your own that you have to live with, at the end of the day. Make sure it's something you can sleep about, at night. Don't operate, in vain glory or puffiness. Pride comes before a fall and those bumps do hurt. You must learn to stand on your own, because the majority will have their vote, but you are the owner. When things come back around, your name is on that paperwork and every situation can have good or bad consequences. If anything, remember, even when you think no one is looking, God sees all and knows all and is always watching!

<u>A TIME TO REFLECT</u>

WHAT ARE SOME THINGS YOU NEED TO AVOID, TO FOCUS
MORE ON BRINGING YOUR BUSINESS TO LIFE?

_____

_____

_____

_____

_____

LIST SEVERAL PEOPLE THAT YOU WOULD ENTRUST YOUR
BUSINESS TO IN YOUR ABSENCE AND A TRAIT YOU WOULD
WANT THEM TO HAVE FROM YOU?

1. _____

    _____

2. _____

    _____

3. _____

    _____

Is there anyone that you need to forgive or apologize to? If so, give them a call and do it now or pray to God about it, so He can lift that dead weight off of you and give you your life back.

<u>*PRAYER*</u>

FATHER, THANK YOU FOR DYING FOR ME, SO THAT I CAN HAVE EVERLASTING LIFE. ALLOW MY ACTIONS AND CONVERSATION TO BE PLEASING TO YOU. I MIGHT NOT DO EVERYTHING RIGHT ALL THE TIME, BUT BY READING YOUR WORD DAILY AND APPLYING YOUR PRINCIPLES TO MY LIFE, I AM DOING BETTER. MOLD ME INTO THE WOMAN OF GOD THAT YOU DESIRE ME TO BE AND USE ME, AS YOUR VESSEL FOR YOUR SERVICE AS A LEADER. IN JESUS NAME, AMEN,

"Ten Steps" To Start a Business

1. **_MY NICHE'-_** First, you must decide on what you want your business to be. Is it a service like shoe repair, brake shop, ice cream parlor or hair salon? You have to make that decision and not depend on other people to decide for you. Of course, they can offer their advice or opinion, but you should always have the final say and definitely pray about it. At the end of the day, your name is on the paperwork and all rewards or issues will be yours to handle, whether good or bad.

2. **_LOCATION-_** What area do you want to service? East, West, North or South, International or Domestic? Do you need to be in a place where there is a lot of foot traffic? Will you keep your doors locked, during normal business hours for safety? Are you comfortable with entering and leaving your business at different times of the day and are your customers safe? Depending on what type of business will determine your area. Also with technology being so broad, you can conduct business meetings and negotiate contracts right from your kitchen, in Detroit, way over to Tokyo.

Find out who and what your target market is and figure out your demographics for age, sex, and groups you would like to impact. Be careful not to discriminate and make it accessible to all.

3. ***LEGACY-*** Think of a creative name that will be respected and honored, even after you have passed. Your goal is to build an empire and leave a legacy. It should be a name that is quick to catch on to and can be abbreviated, but still make sense. Your name always works, because you are the one starting the business and once again your business should represent you.

4. ***REGISTER YOUR BUSINESS NAME-*** Once you have created the name of your business, it's time to pay and register it, so it's yours to keep and no one else's business can be called that name. Depending on the type of business entity you are setting up, you'll have to register it with a county clerk in your State or the Department of Licensing and Regulatory Affairs, or LARA. There are many options of registering your name as a Sole proprietorship, Corporation, or a LLC-limited liability company. You might want to start a not for profit also known as operating a Non-Profit Organization with or without a 501c3. You can reserve a name, while in the process of setting up the business by filing an Application for Reservation of Name form with the state. Trademark Infringement can be checked by searching the federal trademark registry, before filing your application to make sure you are not infringing on a trademark owned by another business.

5. **_OBTAIN A TAX ID NUMBER-_**   Every business must have a tax ID number and pay taxes, in some sort of way. Business taxes, personal taxes, property taxes, sales tax or withholding taxes. A federal tax ID number (also known as an employer identification number or EIN) is solely assigned to you by the IRS. This number helps to identify your business to federal agencies and any business offering products or services that are taxed in any way must get a federal ID number and plan to file yearly taxes.

6. **_BUSINESS PLAN-_**   Create a great business plan and seek help, if needed. Help can be found online or at local business and community centers. You can also hire and pay a professional to put one together for you or talk to a college and see if students in business classes can help you develop one to earn extra credit for coursework. Also, use your computer resources and search engines, for step by step directions on writing a business plan.

7. **_FINANCES-_** If you have savings and are able to open your business without a loan that is the route you should take. Depending on the business or non-profit, you can even set up a Go-fund me account where people donate to you for the cause you are starting. When I first opened, I was blessed with a small grant to start up the business at home and used some of my 401K. Some people begin business ventures with inheritance money from a passed love one, prize money, and retirement or just use funds they have actually already saved. The idea is to remain debt-free, so when the money from your business begins to come you can save that and enjoy it or franchise into

other areas. Also, make sure you pay yourself and keep track with a paper trail of draws from your business bank account, where bank statements can be produced.

8. ***COMPETITION-*** Knowing your competition is very important. I often stay focused on my business, but it's always good to see what the next business is doing, because you can stay ahead of the game and relevant. Try to offer goods and services that are meaningful. Don't ever think things are too crazy, because it may be just right for the consumer. Restaurants, gas stations, stores, beauty salons, daycares, boutiques even churches are on every corner, but the key is you may have and offer something that the other businesses don't. There is no perfect business and everyone offers different services. It could be later hours, free cheese on the burger or the gift wrapping with your boutique purchase, but whatever it is let it be something that allows your business to stand out from the rest.

9. ***ADVERTISING-*** This is one of the main things that will help, in getting your business booming. With Social Media like Facebook, Instagram or Twitter, you can basically advertise for free! The traditional flyers, commercials, billboards and word of mouth are also very useful tools. Other ways to advertise are car decals, T-shirts, hats, jackets, ads in the local paper or church bulletins and school newsletters. Branding yourself with a cool logo and color scheme is important and even if you use black and white, just make sure everything always matches. The signage, social media pages, notepads, letterhead, business cards and all marketing materials

should represent your company and be noticeable, as soon as you see it. A company website that's only a click away will also notify customers of sales, events and discounts offered plus coupons. Mc Donald's is known for their golden arches and Victoria's Secret is known for their wings. What will you be known for?

10. **_TEAMWORK_**- It's very important to pray for a strong, dependable and trustworthy team! The idea is for them to help you make your business operate effectively, even if you are not there. When staffing, pray for leaders that have a heart and genuine concern about you and your business and that honesty is at the top of their list when it comes to giving you daily reports. It's sad to say in today's society a lot of people only want a paycheck or a job. You want to have people on your team that have a passion to help your business grow and are an asset not a liability to your company. A lot of businesses go under, because their team is not strong enough to help the company sustain and only have a me mentality. As a leader of your business, be sure to get educated and hardworking individuals to help run your business. You need people that are teachable and don't have the I know it all already attitude. I was blessed to have some team players, at my business that rolled with me through the valleys and the mountains and understood the dry seasons and the overflow. Most businesses have dry patches and some are always in surplus. Employees often blame the employers, when the business slows down or the economy is bad and they must cut hours. That's why you must be friendly, but not friends with employees. It makes it easier when handling company

issues and concerns and helps to not mislead people. When you first open, you or a manager that knows your dreams and vision must always be around to make sure the business is operating smoothly and must lead by example. That means, as the owner, you can't come to work late, unprepared or under the influence. But, be consistent always, in a leadership position. Pray for the right people to be on staff to help you, so in your absence your business can still prosper. Use people with integrity, trustworthy and the ability to use confidentiality, as they see you do the same. I was once told that your business should have someone in it that is a duplicate of you, so if you can't be there people will never be able to tell. Ask yourself, who am I molding into me for the future of my company? My mother always told me you don't have a successful business, until it can run itself even if you are absent. It honestly took me about 2 years to see my business run on its own and God led me to my next business venture into a building that I wasn't even looking for at the time to expand. I was comfortable in my basement, knew all the parents of my daycare and was excited about being at home with my son. But, my family told me that I was a light that couldn't be kept hidden in the basement and just like that I took that step out on faith to open up the daycare facility. I quickly went from an employer of one employee to a team of eight. I constantly praise God daily, for my staff, and always walk on the saying, "It takes TEAMWORK TO MAKE THE DREAMWORK!"

A TIME TO REFLECT

WHAT NAME WOULD YOU GIVE YOUR BUSINESS AND DRAW
YOUR LOGO BELOW; WHAT WOULD YOUR LOGO LOOK LIKE?

_____

_____

_____

YOUR COMPANY LOGO:

DESCRIBE TEAMWORK IN YOUR OWN WORDS:

_____

_____

_____

_____

PRAYER

FATHER, BEING A BUSINESS OWNER CAN BE A LITTLE FRIGHTENING AT TIMES, BECAUSE OF WHAT I OFTEN SEE WITH MY NATURAL EYES. BUT, YOU ALWAYS REASSURE ME, YOU HAVE MY BACK AND THERE IS NOTHING TO FEAR. FOR YOUR WORD SAYS IN MATTHEW 6:33, "BUT, SEEK FIRST HIS KINGDOM AND HIS RIGHTEOUSNESS AND ALL THESE THINGS WILL BE GIVEN TO YOU AS WELL." (NIV) AND, I WALK ON THAT SCRIPTURE KNOWING THIS BUSINESS BELONGS TO YOU. THANK YOU FOR ALLOWING ME TO TURN IT OVER TO YOU YEARS AGO AND ALLOWING YOU TO TAKE THE WHEEL.

Business Expenses

When operating a business, you will always have expenses and can deduct the majority of them on your yearly taxes. Business expenses are costs you don't have to capitalize and in order to deduct a business expense, they must be ordinary and necessary. Ordinary expenses are common ones that are accepted in the type of business you run and necessary expenses are the ones you need and are adequate for your business.

Start-up Cost

There are a number of expenses, when starting a business. It is best to compile a list such as advertising, travel costs associated with finding suppliers, distributors and customers, consultant fees, employee training and wages and supplies that can all be listed under "start-up" costs and claimed on your taxes. It is important, with all things, to keep good records and a paper trail, for the future.

Insurance

This is one of the main expenses, in every business. Commercial or renter's insurance helps to protect your investment. This includes theft, fire, flood, hazard and accidental insurance. It also protects the customers and worker's compensation protects the employees on the job. If a person is walking outside and trips on a crack, falls and breaks a leg, your insurance can pay their medical expenses, because you pay a yearly insurance. Other insurances are Fidelity (also called bonding) which is used for stores, cleaning services, art dealers and shows that you are trustworthy and won't steal.

Accountant

Another important asset to any company is a solid, honest and trustworthy accountant. They are there to help you keep your books, receipts and business affairs in order. In case you have an audit by the IRS or anyone, an accountant can produce monthly profit and loss statements, quarterly reports and yearly tax returns. They can handle your payroll, address concerns with the Unemployment Agency and any issues that arise regarding the financial part of your business. Your accountant can handle many of the finances for you which, in return, allow you time to focus on other areas of your business. It's vital that you review and plan sit down meetings, with your accountant, so that you know where your money is being allocated and how the company is actually doing. Don't get to busy and uninterested with the business, so that you lose focus and end up losing your business.

Taxes & Inspection Fees

Regardless if you rent or own your business, you will occur some type of tax fee. The various taxes are federal, state, local and foreign taxes. Owners of property have property taxes on the land and actual building or home. Renters also accrue fees, due to personal property taxes, which are taxes paid on the equipment inside of the property. Such as toys, equipment, supplies or whatever is needed to run the business. Inspection fees can range from $350.00 for fire inspections, $425 for Lead inspections, $100 for furnace inspections, $250 for building and $300 for city environmental inspections. It depends on the size of the building or home and the type of inspection that is needed to pass and gain a certificate of occupancy. Without the correct certificates showing your facility has passed, you run the risk of your business being fined and closed down, until obtained.

Mortgage Expense/Rent Expense

Mortgage is the amount you pay to a lending company or a bank to pay them for your property, until it is paid in full and then you are free from the debt. But, you are still required to pay the taxes on the property and the land. Rent is the amount you pay, for the use of the property that you don't own. Some landlord's only sign a three to five year lease to secure a consistent tenant in their property. Other landlords are more understandable and will allow you to do a month to month lease verses a yearly lease. It depends on what the owner of the building wants to do at that time. They may just want a tenant in it, so vandals won't damage their property. You can also ask for a discount or waived first month rent, until you move in to start making a profit. It doesn't hurt to ask, because some buildings are move in ready and some require special licensing, inspections and equipment. Make sure you read the entire lease and hire an attorney to review your lease with you. Point out any discrepancies on the lease and return to the landlord for answers prior to signing. Take it back to your attorney, for a final review. Be careful, because some leases have automatic renewals built into the contracts and if you don't notify the landlord you are moving out at the end of your lease, they can hook you for another three years. A signature makes that paper a binding agreement, for the dates on the paper, and you are responsible for the debt. No matter if the business is closed and goes under, your name is on there and most landlords generally have you sign leases as a personal guarantor, meaning you the individual will be responsible for payment not the company. So, if the business goes under you can be sued and payment will be demanded from you directly. Always pay rent in the form of a check, money order, cashier's check or credit card, so you can always have a paper trail. Obtain your landlord's EIN number, so you can claim this amount when you file your taxes. When repairs or issues arise at your location, be sure to address immediately and also check your lease to see who's responsible for plumbing, fixtures, electrical and repairs.

Security

With the ever rising threats on society, security is important to have for your business. The kind of security you decide on all depends on what kind of business you are operating. Will you have armed or unarmed security, for the protection of your customers and staff or cameras and mirrors to view predators as they come and leave? You can also use the ever sturdy bars, locks and barb wires to keep thieves from coming inside your facility. Most insurance companies give discounts, if you have an alarm system that reports directly to the police or fire department automatically. Whatever you choose, never think that there is no one watching for an opportunity to strike, when you are not there.

Landscaping & Property

Depending on the size of your business, lawn care and snow removal can be maintained in house or you may find it easier to pay a company to handle this expense. It is important to keep a polished and cleaned look for your business that will draw customers in. That means clean windows, walkways, manicured lawns and clear paths from snow, ice and debris to eliminate the chances of falls or injuries.

Grand Opening

You have completed your checklist and now it's time to let the world know you are OPEN FOR BUSINESS! This is a very important day for you and your team and all that hard work, preparation, blood, sweat and tears are over. Depending on what type of business it is, some people have a soft opening two weeks prior with family and friends to work out all the small kinks. If it's a restaurant or service, you want to look at the time the customer waited to get their food or items brought out to them. You also want to make sure you have change on site, extra bags and great customer service. What steps would you take, if your register went down or was frozen? How do you handle an irate customer? These are all things to take into consideration when you do your grand opening. Yes, the easy part is done, the balloons, food and music but what about the distractions or issues. Is the manager prepared to handle them, all at once? Sit down with your staff and talk over the good, bad and the ugly, from the soft opening and receive suggestions and make corrections. Start over and plan for your Grand Opening two weeks to one month later correcting everything on the list.

If nothing went wrong, great, but you should always plan ahead just in case something does not go the way you planned.

These are just a few of the expenses listed which goes along with the daily, weekly or monthly expenses of a business such as the following:

UTILITIES- (WATER,LIGHTS, GAS, PHONE,)	CHARITABLE DONATIONS(CHURCH,SCHOOLS)
SUPPLIES (OFFICE/CLEANING)	SECURITY
PAYROLL	ENVIRONMENTAL SERVICES(TRASH/RECYCLING)
GAS/CAR REPAIRS	POSTAGE
FOOD	TITHES
HEALTH INSURANCE	TRAVEL & ENTERTAINMENT
ADVERTISING	LEGAL & PROFESSIONAL SERVICES
INTEREST	BANKING FEES
REPAIR & MAINTENANCE	LANDSCAPING & PROPERTY MANAGEMENT

A TIME TO REFLECT

DO YOU THINK YOU CAN GET AROUND TO AVOIDING SOME OF THE EXPENSES LISTED ABOVE? IF SO, HOW AND WHICH ONE WOULD YOU CHOOSE?

_____

_____

_____

_____

_____

WHAT ARE SOME OF THE START UP COSTS, FOR YOUR BUSINESS?

_____

_____

_____

_____

_____

<u>*PRAYER*</u>

FATHER, YOU ARE SUCH A GOOD, GOOD FATHER AND I THANK YOU FOR EVERY EXPENSE AND THE FUNDS TO PAY THEM, MONTHLY. THAT LET'S ME KNOW THAT I'M DOING SOMETHING RIGHT, WHEN THE BUDGET IS BEING HANDLED. CONTINUE TO LET MY BUSINESS BE IN SURPLUS, AS I GROW HIGHER IN YOU. IN JESUS NAME, AMEN.

Chapter Seven

Get To It & Do It

Now that you have the basic steps to getting your business started, it's time to start fresh. Dig out that notebook with those bright ideas, witty inventions and grandma's homemade pound cake recipe! Pray and fast about your business, for direction from God and start planning to bring it to fruition. Place all your fears and doubts behind you and trust yourself to do a great job. Life is trial and error and so is business. Don't doubt, but believe in yourself and know that Hebrews 13:21 says, "God will equip you with every good thing to do His will, working in us what is pleasing before Him through Jesus Christ, to whom be glory forever." (NIV) Meaning, God will provide you with the resources to get the job done. So, believe in yourself, if nobody else does. You now know you will have 3 cheerleaders, in your corner, supporting, yourself, God and Me! It's nothing to **IT,** but to do **IT**, so go from a Busy Woman to a Business Woman today!

PRAYER

FATHER, I FEEL I AM READY AND EQUIPPED WITH KNOWLEDGE TO GO OUT AND CHANGE THE WORLD WITH MY GIFTS, ABILITIES AND TALENTS. HELP OTHERS TO SEE THE GLORY OF YOU IN ME AND LET MY LIFE BE A LIVING TESTIMONY OF YOU WITH SKIN ON SHARING THE LOVE FOR PEOPLE TO BE MADE WHOLE WITH THE SERVICES I PROVIDE. IN JESUS NAME I PRAY, AMEN.

Notes

_____

_____

_____

_____

_____

_____

_____

_____

_____

_____

_____

_____

_____

_____

_____

_____

_____

_____

_____

_____

_____

_____

_____

_____

About The Author

Born and educated in Detroit, Catrina successfully earned degrees in business, childcare and non-profit leadership from Madonna and Wayne State University. She has 16 years of experience in entrepreneurship and marriage. Her skills and expertise, as an ordained Deaconess, life coach, philanthropist, and personal stylist, has inspired many. Motivational speaking, acting, dancing and modeling only broaden and enhance her gifts of creativity. Catrina is the owner of Cole's Castle Learning Center of Performing Arts, THRONE by Catrina Maria Boutique and the founder of The Royalty Foundation. These businesses and organizations are used to educate, build, strengthen and empower people of all ages from all walks of life. She was honored, by Ms. Oprah Winfrey, as a Community Hero in 2010 for her generous heart and scholarships given to kids in need. She is the founder of Proms for Mom's. Catrina focuses on inspiring others to be the best that they can be, has a humble heart and a giving spirit that connects and embraces the lives and dreams of people wherever she goes.